My Spirit, My Journey

A Beginner's Guide: How to discover, decide, and delight in your spiritual journey

Theresa Williams

ISBN: 0692575529

ISBN-13: 978-0692575529

DEDICATION

This book is dedicated to my parents and grandparents, who are perfect examples of unconditional love.

This book is dedicated to my wonderful friends. Thank you for your support and patience.

This book is dedicated to the beautiful souls who shared their knowledge, experiences, and vulnerability in order for me to make this book a reality.

CONTENTS

INTRODUCTION

In the Beginning

When I think back to the point I consider my spiritual journey first starting, I remember having a lot of questions. I didn't know who I should ask, what I should ask, or if I should even be asking. I did a lot of reading, asking more questions, more reading, listening to podcasts, and watching webinars. I thought, "Gee, I wish there were some sort of book I can read that had the answers to all my questions in one place". I realized the questions would never end. There would always be something new to discover and explore.

Spiritual, to me, doesn't necessarily mean religious, but does not exclude it, either. It is being peaceful, mindful, aware, loving, grateful. A belief of oneness and unity. Being and doing for our highest good. To some, the psychic realm comes into this definition as well.

If you look it up in the dictionary, you may see something such as this:

spiritual [**spir**-i-choo-*uh* l] adjective

of, relating to, or consisting of spirit; incorporeal.

of or relating to the spirit or soul, as distinguished from the physical nature: *a spiritual approach to life.*

closely akin in interests, attitude, outlook, etc.: *the professor's spiritual heir in linguistics.*

of or relating to spirits or to spiritualists; supernatural or spiritualistic.

characterized by or suggesting predominance of the spir it; ethereal or delicately refined: *She is more of a spiritual type than her rowdy brother.*

of or relating to the spirit as the seat of the moral or reli gious nature.

of or relating to sacred things or matters; religious; dev otional; sacred.

of or belonging to the church; ecclesiastical: *lords spiritual and temporal.*

of or relating to the mind or intellect.

You might feel kind of alone, especially when you're first seeking answers. I did! It helps quite a bit to know the experience of other people, what their questions were, and what answers they found. Questions such as:

What is a spiritual journey?

Why do people see things, hear things, know things?

Are there others like me out there?

How do I know what's right for me?

How come some people are so happy with their lives?

Who do I ask about this?

Am I crazy?

What's with these weird dreams?

Is there some way to figure out what my purpose is?

Answers to these questions and more can be found in this book. Think of it as a friendly guide, pointing you in a direction for you to see what adventures await you. I asked 23 wonderful people to share their fears, questions and experiences regarding their spiritual journey. Within that small number, the group is diverse while remaining intimate. I gathered information from men and women, ranging in age from 20's to 60's. From fellow newbies to people who have been aware of the whole 'spiritualness' thing for a very long time. Everyone from students to shamans--from the West Coast to Wisconsin, and Minnesota to Maryland. I'll share experiences of real people, and tell you some places to find support and encouragement.

Although I can't provide you all the answers, I can provide some options to explore which will take you down what ever path you choose. There is no right or wrong. Your path is determined by what resonates with you.

You can read the chapters in order, or skip around as you desire. Either way, you'll find support, learn something new, and help in choosing the best spiritual path for you. Excited? Me too! Let's go!

CHAPTER 1

IS IT ME, OR EVERYONE ELSE?

What are the things that make you wonder? Have you always felt different from everyone else, like an outsider? Have you either felt you have special gifts or has someone told you that you have gifts? Maybe you feel a deep connection with others, with the earth, to the angels, or the Divine. Do you have dreams about things that will happen, and then they do? Have you always had an inner knowing? Perhaps you grew up in a family that had regular spiritual practices, and you are now finding out that everyone is not like that.

Unless you've been raised with some knowledge of these types of things, you may think you've lost your mind. For example, you tell your coworker there was a ghost in the ladies room and she recommends you get your head checked. You ask your brother, "Where is that music coming from?", and he says, "What music?". Everyone at church seems very touched by the sermon, but you feel that something is missing from it.

I grew up feeling like I didn't fit in. I believed in God, but I didn't know how a God who could love us no matter what could also be so harsh. I noticed in my teen years I would think about things or events and then they would happen. I always had an inner voice or knowing of some kind if something was or wasn't right. If I mentioned this to my friends, they thought I was off my rocker. So, I kept quiet. I buried that part of me away for many years. I got to a point where I was very unhappy, and just figured that's how the rest of my life would be. Then, somehow, I stumbled across a webinar about the Law of Attraction. If you don't know about the Law of Attraction, the shortest definition I can give you is; ask, believe, receive. I found it very interesting, and was eager to learn more. The webinar host had suggested watching the movie, "The Secret".

The first time I watched "The Secret", I only made it about 20 minutes into the movie. I thought, *This is bullshit. You don't just throw it out there that you want something and it magically falls into your lap.* I sent the movie back to Netflix. A few months went by, and I read more about the Law of Attraction, listened to some podcasts, started reading about angels, and started meditating. I was really starting to understand the process now, and how much control I really have in the things that go on in my life. It was time to watch "The Secret" again.

I listened closer now, and they said some things that, had I listened more intently the first time, could have been clearer to me much sooner. I was too closed off before to hear it. They say when the student is ready, the teacher appears. This student was not ready the first time.

Once I finally decided it was up to me, not everyone else, to decide what makes me happy, I knew I had to learn more about how to get to a state of peacefulness. I was tired of always having that nagging feeling of knowing there was something better than just existing. I wanted to get up in the morning and feel good about my life and the things that were going on in it. Back then, it was much easier to give you a list of things that weren't going well.

I spent all my spare time reading, listening to podcasts, webinars, anything and everything I could find about how to live in a way that would make me happiest. One of the hundreds of websites I looked at showed an advertisement for a Holistic Healing and Psychic Expo coming to a town very near me. Wow! I was going, no matter what. I had to see what this was all about. I hadn't mentioned to any of my friends that I was "into this weird Law of Attraction and meditation stuff" so I went alone. It was *so* fun! I bought incense, had a numerology reading, and listened to several speakers. I had a great time and met people I felt an instant connection with. Of course, with all this new knowledge, there were more things to look into! Things I hadn't heard of yet-more things I may be interested in!

Being a kid, I was 'smart', 'shy', I did as I was told, but (also) always rebelled. I always felt lost spiritually until my husband's mother introduced us to 'Abraham-Hicks' and he and I both started practicing.

~Ashley

I have always been interested in metaphysical topics, and have been drawn to stones and jewelry since I was a child. It wasn't until a trip to Hawaii in 2008 that I realized I could sense and feel the energies of stones.

There was a series of events while there that led me to the person who would show me how to listen to the stones. Since then, I have learned to listen more to my intuition, trust my inner voice and overall be more aware.

~Sara

I always remember being fascinated with angels and the paranormal. When I was in my teens, I started having very vivid dreams, and then eventually they were dreams that came true. In my teens/early adulthood, I started sensing spirit, and just 'knowing' when they were around. I would get random feelings that would urge me to make certain decisions, or say certain things. All of my friends would be creeped out!

~Rachel

I was standing with a group of friends, when a man approached dressed in dirty clothes. He walked directly up to me and said 'You have a huge aura. It's almost as big as mine.' The man simply walked away. My jaw dropped, and immediately I was filled with a million questions. I almost ran after him to ask, 'What does that mean?!' Now I ask myself that question every single day. It's really helped me find purpose.

~Jessica

I have always been different and so that was in some essence a 'normal' feeling for me. However, it was something that I tried to hide (in general) and to just try and blend into the background. I started to realize I was able to access my gifts easily and help others when I took a beginning psychic development class. It helped put all of the pieces together and made me realize that all of the question marks I had about myself were actually gifts to be used. It changed not only the quality of my own life, but later has helped me to assist others on their own spiritual paths.

~Bert

When you read this book, you can investigate what spiritual direction you are interested in taking, find out more about it, and learn how to connect with other like-minded individuals and groups for support. All you have to do is take action on the information provided. (Tips will be given!)

I'd like you to keep your mind open as you read so you may be welcoming to something that is showing up for you just when you need it. This is no coincidence-this is called synchronicity. You'll get the most out of this if you take action on the things that really resonate with you.

The question, again. Is it you, or is it everyone else? The answer: Yes. I'm not trying to mess with you. What I'm saying is, everyone has their own beliefs. You may agree with some people, and disagree with others. We are living on the same planet, at least for now, so we really need to not only be at peace with ourselves, we need to let others be at peace with themselves in their chosen way. Respect each other's right to happiness. Love each other. Learn from each other. Next, let's dig into 'Who, What, When, Where, Why and How'.

CHAPTER 2

WHAT IS THIS ALL ABOUT?

In this chapter, I'll share examples of some things one might be curious about when first realizing their connection to Spirit, or just hearing some of the information for the first time. I'll also cover the Clair senses (sort of the 'psychic match' to our 5 senses) a little later in the chapter.

Now, when I talk about a connection to 'Spirit', I don't mean *spirits*, as in ghosts. (One may also connect with spirits, however.) To me, Spirit is a feeling of oneness, connection, pure love and joy. Personally, I believe in God, but wouldn't label myself 'religious'. When you feel connected, it may be with God, Buddha, the Divine, the Universe, whatever feels good to you to call that Source that makes you feel love, feel joy, feel alive!

8

Some of you may also experience psychic connections. This could be new to you, or perhaps you are just finding out what you've been experiencing all your life you are now able to put a name to.

Let's see what we can find out!

Who am I connecting with/hearing/seeing?

As I mentioned above, you may be connecting with God, Source, The Universe, whatever you choose to call it. You will know you are connected because of the deep peace and unconditional love you feel.

You could also be connecting with spirit guides. Everyone has spirit guides, from the time their soul first existed. Some guides may be with you your entire physical life, and some may be temporary or come and go at different times in your life.

A spirit guide is typically the soul of someone who has, in the past, had a physical existence. Before you come to be in your physical body, you have made a 'plan' of what it is you wish to learn and/or experience in your physical life. (Sometimes known as your Soul's Contract.)

Your spirit guides are there to assist you in staying your course. You may connect with a spirit guide during meditation, or through intuitive nudges you experience, even in a fully aware state. Some folks see and/or hear their spirit guides during meditations.

Another possibility is connecting with angels. We all have angels watching over us! Connection with angels is sometimes confirmed by hearing ringing in the ear(s), hearing music, seeing light anomalies, or possibly even seeing what is perceived as a physical being, sometimes with wings. Your angels love you and wish to assist you in every way possible! They need to be asked, however, in order to assist you. They are eager to spring into action and only await your request. The only time they would step in without being asked is in a life-threatening situation, such as a car wreck. Be sure to thank your angels after asking for help.

Some people are able to connect with spirits on the other side, the deceased. They may hear, see, speak to, or channel someone who has passed. Those who can make connection with someone who is no longer physically on earth are called *mediums.* Being a psychic and being a medium are not the same. Psychics cannot necessarily communicate with the deceased. Mediums definitely do. You may connect with a spirit you know, or someone you do not.

If you feel uneasy with a spirit trying to connect with you, ask it to leave. You are in charge of who you connect with. Some spirits are very talkative and want to give you lots of information, others are a bit more shy.

What did I do to cause this to happen?

Good question! There are many answers.

You've done nothing to make this happen. You've always had some kind of connection, it's just stronger for some than others.

It might be part of your culture, or perhaps others in your family were/are very open about spirituality and you're just now curious to learn more about what has been discussed.

You've had a near death experience, and since then you just feel 'different' about so many things.

Someone very close to you has passed away, and you see and/or speak to them in dreams (you may not be sure if it is a dream or reality).

You've noticed a friend or relative who always seems so peaceful, unshaken, like they are surrounded by love and light. You want to know their secret.

Where does this come from?

This comes from being *aware*.

We get so much input every day, from so many sources. Television, newspaper, radio, magazines, friends, family, co-workers. If your brain tried to analyze all the input you got, you'd certainly go mad getting it all sorted out. We can hear all they are saying, but only certain things catch our attention. We are *aware* of these things, focus on them, and let the rest slide.

You're reading this book because the things you are *aware* of now are different than they were in the past. You pick up on things you didn't before. New and different subjects are sparking your interest.

Why is this happening to me?

To me, the best answer is this; 'When the student is ready, the teacher will appear'. You were not ready to know before. That is why this is happening now. It's why you are seeing, hearing, being told certain things.

Each of us has a definite purpose in life. If you don't know or are confused about what your purpose is, it is difficult to understand why things happen 'to you'. Although we all have free will, we have a path in life, and decisions we make along the way determine if we stay on our path or stray, and if so, how far we do.

Be open to learning more about what is happening and how to work with it to your advantage. This allows you to find out what you need to do to get back on track instead of feeling like a victim.

How do I control it?

It depends on what you mean by control. If you mean to make sure things go a certain way, no matter what, you are setting yourself up for disappointment. Control means being flexible. Control means living in a way that makes you feel good by being able to take what comes your way, keeping and using what resonates with you, and let go what doesn't resonate.

To get good at anything takes practice. The more you practice, the better control you have. If you are psychic or a medium, you may need to practice learning how to control being psychically open, or how/when/where you receive information.

The following are a sampling of the answers I got when I asked my group what they wanted to know first when discovering this area of their life.

It wasn't until later on in life, with my children and the circumstances/stress around me, that I started to remember, question again, and know this wasn't how life was intended to be. I just knew I was missing something. I have always loved to learn. I wanted to know how to fix the stress, the health of my child and husband at the time. To be happy and fulfilled again.

~Kathy

I want to stay aware of as much as possible so that I can learn whatever it is I need to learn for today!

~Toria

I wanted my left brain (the logical part) set at ease, because a lot of this was so outside my normal way of thinking as a doctor and an educator. I wanted reassurance that I wasn't going crazy!

~Lori

If I was crazy! Why, or how this was happening to me, and how could I use it to help others?

~Rachel

I wanted to understand why and how I knew things. I could see, hear, feel and know things. I was very sensitive empathetically. I wanted to understand myself and my own abilities. Some things frightened me about myself.

~Angel

I wanted to know how to be free from my miserable state of being. This was my primary drive. I had no names for what I was feeling, I only knew I was miserable, and wished every day since puberty that I wasn't here, that I was dead. I didn't even think I knew whether it was possible to be joyful or happy from the core of my being.

~Julianna

I was always fascinated with history, but could never remember any of the details. Past lives peaked my interest. Being a skeptic, I questioned whether they were real or not; however, I would have many dreams with people I knew in settings that were historic. There were no details in the dreams of history, I just knew.

~Nicole W.

I really had no desire to understand any of it further. I know that sounds weird, but I wasn't drawn to explore this element of myself at all. Sure, I was intrigued, but exploring this and labeling myself as gifted-or dare I say psychic-meant that I had to place a neon sign in my front window and be what I thought a psychic was, based upon stereotypes. Ghosts were something that intrigued me and I really wanted to understand them.

~Eric

When I finally discovered what an Empath was, I wanted to know everything! I was doing research on the internet non-stop and seeing if it all made sense to me., All of the attributes of an empath was what I was! I also wanted to know more about how to block out those feelings that I did not want to take over. That was the hardest thing for me to do, and what I struggled with a lot before I found out what kind of power I had obtained.

~Nicole S.

What I really wanted to know is why people would choose to treat each other so poorly in life and yet say they love you. How I was raised, there was a lot of confusion for me around love and expression. I think I am figuring it out so I can hold peace inside even when life gets tricky.

~Amy

I was always very intuitive-I could read people easily. I also had many dreams and daydreams (as a child) of past life memories. I just thought they were my imagination. Looking back now, they felt so real (because they were)! Also, connecting with spirit or souls on the other side has always come very naturally to me-I assumed everyone could do it.

~Bert

Rocks...definitely rocks. That started for me when I was about 15. I could feel the energy and knew they all meant something. I discovered how special they were on so many levels.

~Christy

The Clairs-Psychic Match To Our 5 Earthly Senses

According to Wikipedia, definition of the Clairs is as follows:

Clairvoyance (seeing): The term clairvoyance (from French *clair* meaning "clear" and *voyance* meaning "vision") is used to refer to the ability to gain information about an object, person, location or physical event through means other than the known senses, i. e., a form of **extrasensory perception**. A person said to have the ability of clairvoyance is referred to as a clairvoyant ("one who sees clearly").

Clairsentience (feeling/touching): In the field of parapsychology, clairsentience is a form of extra-sensory perception wherein a person acquires psychic knowledge primarily by feeling. The word "clair" is French for "clear", and "sentience" is derived from the Latin sentire, "to feel". Psychometry is related to clairsentience. The word stems from *psyche* and *metric*, which means "soul-measuring".

Clairaudience (hearing/listening): In the field of parapsychology, clairaudience [from late 17th century French *clair* (clear) and audience (hearing)] is a form of extra-sensory perception wherein a person acquires information by paranormal auditory means. It is often considered to be a form of clairvoyance. Clairaudience is essentially the ability to hear in a paranormal manner, as opposed to paranormal seeing (clairvoyance) and feeling (clairsentience).

Clairalience (smelling): Also known as clairescence. In the field of parapsychology, Clairalience (or alternatively, clairolfactance) [presumably from late 17th century French *clair* (clear) and alience (smelling)] is a form of extra-sensory perception wherein a person accesses psychic knowledge through the physical sense of smell.

Claircognizance (knowing): In the field of parapsychology, claircognizance [presumably from late 17th century French *clair* (clear) and *cognizance* (< ME *cognisaunce* < OFr *conoissance*, knowledge)] is a form of extra-sensory perception wherein a person acquires psychic knowledge primarily by means of intrinsic knowledge. It is the ability to know something without a physical explanation why you know it, like the concept of mediums.

Clairgustance (tasting): In the field of parapsychology, clairgustance is defined as a form of extra-sensory perception that allegedly allows one to taste a substance without putting anything in one's mouth. It is claimed that those who possess this ability are able to perceive the essence of a substance from the spiritual or ethereal realms through taste.

Questions and answers provide the opportunity for more questions and, fortunately, more answers! The best way to make sure you find out what you want to know is ask! Next, let's take a look at some of the places we can find some answers.

CHAPTER 3

WHO DO I TALK TO ABOUT THIS?

If you're like me, the more you know, the more you want to know. If a topic resonates with me, I will try all kinds of resources and get more information, until my curiosity has been satisfied. I think I can safely say very few of us has a guru living next door to ask questions that come up.

Where do we go for answers? There are many resources. I suggest mixing it up a bit. Don't Google everything. Talk to some real live people, read a book, go to a meeting, all of the above! By getting answers from more than one resource, you may receive information that really resonates, really gives you the answer you feel in your soul is what you've known all along.

Google is a great place to start, but you get no interaction with it, so I strongly suggest meeting up with another person, or group of people.

The following is certainly not an all-inclusive list of places to seek answers to your questions. It will definitely give you a great start, however!

People

- ❖ Friends
- ❖ Family
- ❖ Co-workers
- ❖ Group members (online or in person)
- ❖ Teachers
- ❖ Psychics/Intuitives
- ❖ Pastor
- ❖ God
- ❖ Mentor
- ❖ Angels
- ❖ Spirit Guides
- ❖ Your Higher Self
- ❖ Elders

Online

I will include a list of links to specific websites later on. Here are some keywords/phrases you can Google that will provide many websites you can peruse.

- ❖ spiritual journey
- ❖ finding peace
- ❖ psychic
- ❖ intuition
- ❖ gratitude
- ❖ healing energy
- ❖ law of attraction
- ❖ vision boards
- ❖ meditation
- ❖ angels
- ❖ spirit guides
- ❖ channeling
- ❖ drum circles
- ❖ mantras
- ❖ elementals
- ❖ fairies
- ❖ source energy
- ❖ soul contract
- ❖ past lives
- ❖ crystals
- ❖ manifesting
- ❖ abundance
- ❖ indigo children
- ❖ holistic
- ❖ EFT (emotional freedom technique)
- ❖ divination
- ❖ smudging
- ❖ angel numbers
- ❖ ascended masters
- ❖ workshops
- ❖ affirmations
- ❖ feminine power
- ❖ retreats

- ❖ inner guidance
- ❖ personal growth
- ❖ empowerment
- ❖ yoga
- ❖ empath
- ❖ Reiki
- ❖ metaphysical
- ❖ aromatherapy
- ❖ spirit animal
- ❖ oracle cards
- ❖ tarot
- ❖ hypnosis
- ❖ astrology
- ❖ numerology
- ❖ dream interpretation
- ❖ positive thinking
- ❖ healing
- ❖ journaling
- ❖ releasing blocks
- ❖ chakras
- ❖ shamanism
- ❖ sacred geometry
- ❖ spiritual books
- ❖ holistic expos
- ❖ auras

There are all sorts of groups on Facebook and many other places online you can join that are specifically for asking questions and receiving support from like-minded people. Finding like-minded people is a HUGE benefit! You learn from others, and they learn from you. Yes, you. You may not think you have knowledge or valuable experience to share, but you do.

Interacting with others who think like you can bring your big 'a-ha!' moment, can make you feel a sense of belonging, can raise your vibration (energy), and give you new knowledge that you may be able to pass along to someone else.

Now that you're starting to get some more information, let's look at how it comes into play when we interact with others.

CHAPTER 4

TO BE, OR NOT TO BE...OR BOTH?

Where I'm from, spirituality is respected and being individual is celebrated.

~Toria

Congratulations, you have discovered a bunch of exciting new information! Do you want to share it with everyone you know, or at the other end of the spectrum, are you afraid to say anything about it to the people you know for fear they will think you've lost your mind? Are you in the spiritual 'closet', out of it, or some combination of both? The answer really depends on you.

I, for the most part, am still very deep in the closet with my gifts. I work in the law enforcement field and as you can imagine, it's not an open field as far as spirituality goes. I do use my gift on a daily basis for my job. When someone asks me how I knew certain information, I reply, 'Oh, it was just a hunch.' My Dad and most extended family have no idea about my gifts. Most people that I do readings for have heard about me through the grapevine. I love doing readings for people I do not know at all. It's a great way to test my gift out.

~Breanna

I do not think I kept my first gift in the closet, but in my culture humility is values, so I do not really talk about it to very many people. However, now that I realize I am psychic and that I am also a medium and a healer, I do not talk about this to many people. I mainly talk to those who know me, those who are also psychic, and my mentors. I definitely do not talk about this to my work colleagues or casual acquaintances.

~Kim S.

The moment I came out of the closet was after I had the opportunity to speak with Sylvia Browne. I told her I thought I was crazy, but more like I was afraid to look or sound crazy' She said to me, 'Keely, do you know how many people think I'm crazy? If you have a message, deliver it.' I was in my late 20's. I slowly began telling people when I would hear their guides and angels speak for their loved ones that have passed on.

~Keely

At first I was eager to tell people. I wanted everyone to know about this new side to life. If I could, they could too! I kept wanting to open people up and find ways of introducing spiritual topics of discussion. I got mixed reactions, but on the whole, people seemed to be limited in their ability to relate to what I was saying. Now I am selectively open about it, but, if I find out someone has an interest in the spiritual, I am usually wide open. It isn't that I wouldn't share it with everyone, but I have found that some people aren't ready to hear the message. Since I physically experience the spiritual, it is a truth for me, and my truths cannot be compromised by someone else's disbelief. So, if I feel comfortable, I will share a lot.

~Jessica

I tell people I am comfortable with. I still work in the corporate world, but over the last year, I have become more comfortable with just putting it out there. People who know me know that I am genuine, and that I'm not just delusional or making things up.

~Rachel

I'm an intuitive, right? So I felt out who to tell and where to keep it to myself. My in-laws still don't know I read. I think they'd be fine with it because on a whole host of levels I've shown them my prowess in the area of wisdom.

~Amy

I began studying shamanism after the death of my son, in seeking to find healing for myself. At the time I also had two teenage daughters and I waited until they graduated from high school to come out of the closet and I have remained out for the past 25 years.

~Jeanne

It depended on the environment or situation I was in, but I found I kept it a little more hidden when I was first starting. As I age, and worry less about the opinions of others, I am finding I am more free with my speech, and am careful to remain respectful of those with differing opinions.

I am also learning to not hold on to what I started with. While I started with crystals, I am now moving on to realize my path is to live authentically and show those around me how to do the same. I am also feeling drawn to empowering others through releasing fear and settling into their own worth. It is an ongoing shift.

~Sara

Being from a Native tribe, we just "are". Your gifts are yours, and life is a lesson. Being/living off the Reservation is different. I try to observe rather than be observed or attract attention. Where I'm from, spirituality is respected and being an individual is celebrated.

~Toria

I would say I started 'somewhere in between'. When I started being public, I hid behind a safe subject-Aromatherapy-incorporating it with my Reiki energy work. I would give information I received during session without fear of completely failing. It helped me to build up my confidence and to blossom my gifts to what they are today, because I listened to my guides and was validated from clients. I believe I walk my talk now, after much work on myself . I visited past lives and cleared much karma. It is interesting to see how much influence they have on how we live our lives today.

I have also worked on this life-my inner child and what she needed to heal.

~Nicole W.

I am exactly the same to you as I am to everybody. For me to hide who I am goes against who I am as a spiritual being. I am comfortable with who I am, what I do and how I live my life. I believe your spiritual path should be a way of life.

~Christy

All in all, it really depends on comfort level. How comfortable are you with your beliefs, your gifts? How comfortable are you with others having their beliefs and gifts, especially if they are different than yours? So simple, yet so complicated! If it feels good, share. If you're not sure, explore.

We are all one.

CHAPTER 5

LIFE HAPPENS-WHAT DO I DO THEN?

I think I still struggle to combine my two beliefs about reality--the one that didn't think this was possible and is still clinging to a normal pick-up-the-dry-cleaning kind of life, and the one that can see that things are not what they had seemed.

~Jessica

How can you deal with life's daily circumstances and challenges? You have this feeling inside you, wanting to live in your truth, wanting joy and abundance. You come out of meditation or leave a meeting of like-minded people, and you are floating on your high vibration. Then, something happens.

The children are fighting, someone cuts you off in traffic, you get a phone call from that perpetually negative relative.

How do we deal with it? If you're not prepared, you can go from 60 to zero pretty fast. One big thing to remember is you cannot control what others say or do, only how you react to it. Sometimes, without even realizing it, we are affected by other's emotions and negativity. Perhaps you are experiencing anger, overwhelm, guilt, or fear of leaving the familiar and trying something new.

It's important to keep your vibration (the energy that flows from you) at the highest level you can. You are more aligned with your path when your vibration is high, and less aligned when it is lower. As Esther Hicks says, if you are feeling negative (lower vibration) emotions, you are paddling your canoe upstream. Seek a better feeling emotion, which then raises your vibration, let go of the oars and float downstream! The Universe is conspiring with you to create circumstances that match the vibe you send out. You send your vibe out to the Universe by the way you feel.

Everyone will feel bad from time to time. You can't go from angry to elated in a few minutes. Just work towards another emotion that makes you feel even a bit of relief, and you are on your way to a higher vibration and feeling better. It's not 'bad' to have negative emotions, they are part of life.

Just don't pitch your tent and live there!

There are many ways to deal with all life's 'stuff'. Stay true to yourself and what feels good in your heart. Do something that makes you feel whole, peaceful, connected.

I try to meditate every morning. However, meditation for me is basically journaling, channeling, or just listening to spirit guide me. This helps set the tone for my day and has been the greatest asset in developing my gifts.

~Bert

For me, it's writing, journaling, channeling from my higher self and my guides. Being able to use my experiences to speak.

~Keely

Meditation, breathing exercises, swimming or sitting in the whirlpool, water therapy, being near water, shielding techniques, burning ritual incense, clearing energy, prayer. I also try to stay connected to Spirit for guidance and knowledge, (and do) daily affirmations.

~Angel

The support of my friends. Just being myself and being true to myself has been helpful.

~Lori

Anything outside-reading, walking, hiking, playing, driving, sitting, thanking. I know I am one with nature and it strengthens me!

~Ashley

I love doing readings with oracle cards. I love when the information starts flowing and my head starts tingling.

~Dakota

My practice fuels and sustains my earthly life. I simply could not exists without it and I truly wonder how people manage day to day without a connection to source wisdom. I have different practices because I am a woman, and I need variety! Some days I sit quietly in meditation. If I have had a dream that needs exploring, I may explore this is meditation or perhaps a shamanic journey feels more appropriate. Anointing myself with my holy oils is essential for me. They help connect me to Spirit, to the beings of the planet realms and offer so much in the way of peace and harmony, and to the general health and well being of my physical body temple. When I have visions or ideas I wish to deepen with, I collage from magazines and dialogue with them.

This is powerful and surprisingly revealing, and draws from the Mystery. Walking in nature and being near water is very valuable as well. And playing! Playing is a MUST! Laughing with loved ones, my sweet dog, Sukha, and the earth. Walking in the woods, I say hello to the trees and plants, and delight when they dance and wave a greeting in return. Sometimes I put on some music and dance with the moon, wild and crazy, or soft and slow. I do what makes my heart and body delight and rest in being here now.

~Julianna

What I do and practice to help me feel my best is daily meditation. I do a Chakra clearing with affirmations on myself daily, exercise and eat healthy. What helps me to stay on my path is maintaining that connection to Source energy. Going into my heart, being conscious of my actions and deeds. Being mindful and loving and honoring myself.

~Tammy

Dance and drawing. Walking in nature, being near water. Sharing time as a family. Acceptance, finding people that appreciate my work. A lot of breath work. Finding like-minded souls.

~Kim B.

Working with and selling rocks is my passion. I am in my bliss state when I am working with people and the energies of stones and how different they are to each individual. Doing aura photos proves that. On an energy spiritual level this is all very fulfilling and keeps me very happy. Knowing what I do is needed, and not just something I do. I help people on a daily basis get themselves into a better or different place.

~Christy

Teaching yoga and staying in the present moment go hand-in-hand with helping me to feel my best. I also connect with like-minded friends. We remind each other, validate and understand thoughts and questions.

~Nicole W.

I try to be grateful every day. I try to stay positive and always look for my lesson(s) in my daily experience. If I'm not doing these things, I feel it. I also meditate and use Native medicines. I've learned to try and recognize the symptoms of straying from my path and when I realize I've gone astray, I know what to do.

~Toria

Self-care is so important and something I continue to struggle with. I know I feel best when I meditate, yet I don't do it as often as would be best for me. I also know how much better I feel when I get enough sleep, exercise and eat well. Yet, I don't always do those things either. In the end, it is an ongoing lesson I am learning and one that has been ingrained in my life quite a bit more than it was 10 years ago. I am making progress and I am happy with that for now!

~Sara

I do many different things. I do kirtan, which is chanting mantras, and this always puts me in a state of bliss. I practice yoga, which helps to calm my mind I daily drum and connect with nature, for she is the real healer.

~Jeanne

I alternate to keep it fresh! Biking, yoga, running, float tank session, infrared sauna, ionic footbath, eating well. My favorite influence in the spiritual arena once said, 'Only meditate 15 minutes a day.' I love this because it goes along with my deep feeling we are here to be human and engage in living, not purely spiritual practice.

~Amy

Kryon. He is an angel to help us through this transition and is channeled through Lee Carroll. I highly recommend him. He has free audio of his messages from his lectures from all over the world. He is giving information for us now. The messages are what is pertaining to us currently.

It is simple, makes sense and gives me great insight, peace. You can Google him or go to kryon.com.

~Kathy

I have recently gotten into chanting. It really helps to calm me down. I also smudge a lot. I intuitively select which herb I need to do this. I commonly use lavender, sage, palo santo, cedar, and incense. I have also been using moon power to manifest, and I keep an abundance grid with gemstones.

~Rachel

I enjoy meditating. I like to visualize being grounded and watching the energy move up and out of my body. I like opening my chakras and visualizing opening up my Crown and Third Eye chakras. Oddly enough, my daughter keeps me on my path. She is very gifted and when I stray too far off the path she pulls me back. I also look forward to workshops that occur from time to time. They help me re-focus and re-energize, as do meet-ups with like-minded people.

~Kim

It all comes back to my dreams again. When my dreams start to get very vivid and clear, I know Spirit is trying to communicate with me and I need to stop and listen. It's hard for me to do readings on myself so dreams are where it begins for me.

~Breanna

My practice. Trusting, trusting the information that is coming through. Being kind to myself, forgiving myself when I choose the path of resistance and allowing myself to begin anew with each breath. Listening and pausing also help me stay on the path. Tuning-in to my emotions and listening to what they are communicating about my well being. Taking time for myself and allowing myself to do the things that bring me joy. Letting go of the need to be busy. Saying yes to those things that shout out a 'Heck ya!' and either letting the rest go or at least pausing until all systems (emotions, physicality, thoughts, Spirit) say GO!

~Erin

There are certainly some common practices, as you can see, such as meditating and being in nature. We all need time to just 'be'. Even if you can only carve out a small block of time here and there during the day, you need that. Some folks like to get up before everyone else in the house and have that quiet time in the morning to meditate, do yoga, write in a journal or do affirmations. See where you can start finding time to 'sneak' in these little respite periods. You don't have to sit cross-legged and chant while burning incense (but you certainly can!). When you're in line at the grocery store, on your lunch break, waiting for a train, letting that frying pan soak in the dishwater, or sorting laundry, stop and notice. Even if you only have time to take a nice, deep breath and send up a silent 'Thank you'.

Remember, if you are just starting to learn or practice something, be patient with yourself. If it resonates with you, stick with it. If you find it doesn't feel like what you need, try something else. Life is about feeling good, and being armed with some feel-good strategies is important when you're feeling off-kilter.

Now that you've got a few tools for dealing with those everyday things that can throw you off, you are ready to forge ahead!

Variety is the spice of life. Learning new things, or a new way of doing things helps you decide what you prefer, and what direction you would like to pursue. The next chapter is chock-full of subjects you can find out more about. Don't hesitate to explore everything that resonates with you! This is _your_ journey!

CHAPTER 6

WHERE CAN THIS JOURNEY TAKE ME?

This chapter is about ideas. There are so many wonderful and beautiful things to explore about spirituality. You will see how it is really right there in front of us all the time, giving us opportunities to be of service, change how we respond to certain situations, and learn to see things from a different perspective.

Below are some keywords and phrases to plug into your favorite search engine and start checking out what interests you. I've also listed a few websites you may find useful. I had so many questions in the beginning, and spent many hours online researching different subjects. I am happy to have found some great newsletters to sign up for, joined some awesome groups, gained much knowledge, and made many new friends, just by starting to search!

These are in no particular order. Pick what resonates with you and start investigating. Enjoy!

setting intentions	hypnosis
natural medicine	spiritual forums
astrology	podcasts
de-cluttering	numerology
connecting with spirit guides	happiness
blogs	articles
courses	seminars
books	rituals
prayer	affirmations
therapies	astral travel
dream interpretation	healing
mediumship	surrender
sacred geometry	spiritual gifts
oracle cards	tarot readings
runes	i-ching
clearer messages	personal power
yoga	meditation

Reiki	past life regression
angels	shamanism
empath	spiritual communities
psychic	vision boards
mastermind groups	mindful eating
self-care	helping others
chanting	drum circles
chakras	dance
channeling	journaling
workshops	animal communication
paranormal	releasing blocks
abundance	setting boundaries
personal growth	empowerment
spiritual growth	spirit guides
crystals	smudging
clearing	grounding
divination	intuition
metaphysical	aromatherapy

power animal	soul mates
EFT (tapping)	source energy
mantras	classes
positive quotes	acupuncture
angel numbers	law of attraction
manifesting	feminine power
ascended masters	fairies
elementals	star children
indigo children	clarity
inner guidance	retreats
expos	meetups
videos	spiritual alignment
gratitude	energy healing

attractyourdesires.com

allspiritual.com

hayhouse.com

blogtalkradio.com

ted.com/topics/personal+growth

abraham-hicks.com

dictionaryofspiritualterms.com

intenders.com

selfhelpontheweb.com

This is just a sampling of what there is to dig into. Depending on where you live, there may also be New Age stores you can go to for classes or workshops, or find a group to join. I believe it is very valuable to have some type of consistent interaction with like-minded people. It feels good to have someone validate you, and you learn from each other.

You can get click happy on the internet and literally spend hours trying to find the answers to all your questions. There is so much information you can never read it all. As time goes by, you'll be more drawn to some things than others. The things you're drawn to are what you are meant to see, hear, know and do. It's easy to get overwhelmed in the beginning, to want to know everything you can, as fast as you can! Next, I'll share some tips and encouragement for you as you begin to navigate your way.

CHAPTER 7

TIPS AND ENCOURAGEMENT

If you're feeling a bit overwhelmed or overloaded at this point, it's OK! The following is the best explanation I've heard that takes the confusion out of what it means to be on a spiritual journey.

This journey is like a cell phone. We know there are no wires, and there are some towers somewhere that the radio waves bounce off of. I know there are different types of phones-old flip phones, iPhones, Tracfones, and some don't even have any phones. I know that there are many different companies-Verizon, AT&T, Sprint, and many different plans-minutes as you go, unlimited text, data, and usage. We may not understand exactly how if there were a group of people in one room with all these different types of phones, different carriers and plans, can ALL make a CALL and CONNECT to whomever from wherever...across town, across the world...

but it works for them all. They connect to whomever they are choosing. It seems kind of incomprehensible, but if it works for each individual with their particular phone, plan and carrier, that is PERFECT and exciting for them!

Same with this journey. It will be perfect for whatever YOU are lead to. It may be different for your closest friend but know that's okay, too. You may not understand how it works, but stay out of judgment and don't buy anything as truth so you can expand everything that comes to you. Know you'll CONNECT to whomever/whatever is PERFECT for YOU! You can't go wrong.

~Kathy

No matter the path you choose, there is no right or wrong way, only the way that feels good to you. It is okay to be different! Everyone is unique, special, and loved. We are all on different paths, yet we are all one. You are not alone!

Here are a few tips-

- notice signs and symbols
- write down your dreams
- find a teacher or mentor
- don't over think-trust yourself
- keep a gratitude journal
- create a sacred space for yourself
- ask questions

- don't compare yourself to others
- take a step in the direction that calls you
- take time for yourself alone
- find like-minded people to talk with
- be open to new ideas

As you move forward, watch for things to show up as signs you are going in the right direction. Things that are called coincidence by most people are synchronistic events that are supposed to happen, they are not merely chance. For example, when I first started 'paying attention', as I call it, I was sure there was no one else in my area that thought like this, let alone anyone I could talk to or ask questions of. Then, I saw an advertisement for a Holistic Healing and Psychic Expo in my area. I just had to go! I was surprised how many people there were, including people I had seen around town. I found out these expos happen twice a year here, so I continued to go.

I can't begin to tell you the difference I feel about so many facets of my life since I have had the opportunity to follow my curiosity and learn that it is okay to be on my own path. I don't have to be what someone else tells me is the right way to be, or follow the masses to be happy. I choose what I believe, what makes me happy and peaceful. I treasure the bonds I have formed with the people I've met as a result of following what feels good and right to me.

I've come to realize there are many people full of love and acceptance who are interested in helping others-not for personal gain, they truly care about other's wellbeing.

Meditate. Join a group. Ask for Divine assistance. Go to a workshop. Look for the lesson. Pay attention to what resonates. Just take a step, even a small one. Enjoy the feeling of accomplishment of that first step! Once you get the ball rolling, the synchronicities start happening. You'll feel better and better, and your vibration will get higher. The possibilities are endless.

I'd like to share some bits of encouragement from my friends-

Remember that it is OK to be different from everyone else. It is actually better! We are more unique and, in the long run, (in my opinion) more humble. It is great to have the gift you have, and it makes you the person you are today! Be proud and stay strong. There are others out there like you!

~Nicole S.

The hardest step you will take is to just start. Stop dabbling and reading and start doing.

~Bert

There has been far too much fighting and religious controversy. We must all come together and conduct in peace and harmony, and learn from one another. There is no one right belief. We grow strong and inspire each other through unity!

~Angel

Notice signs and symbols. These are your guides. Listen. Do you hear something 2 or 3 times; a book title, a comment or word that sparks your curiosity? Follow it. What are your dreams speaking? I spent years unable to feel my heart, but some other part of me was functioning and drawing me towards the places, resources and people I needed to meet to assist me in clearing the debris. Even if you have yet to feel or experience it, TRUST you are not alone, you are being guided. Follow joy, compassion, kindness and gentleness-even if it is but a brief moment of your day-and trust you will receive exactly what you need.

Find teachings, teachers, mentors that help you access your heart and your own authentic power, for only YOU can determine what is the right path towards your awakening. Develop your capacity to enter the unknown. For the only thing that is ever certain is change, and the more we can develop our capacity to sit in the unknown, find stillness in the midst of chaos, the greater our capacity to move with shifting times.

Lastly, this journey is not meant to be walked alone or in isolation. Find your tribe, connect with a being or beings who validate and support your BECOMING, your THRIVING, and inspire love in your heart. For much of my adult life, this was an elder who needed assistance. I used to wonder why I liked old people so much. I came to understand that they could love me no matter what. They also gave me an opportunity to show up with my kind and gentle loving self, most critical in my life when I could not show up this way for myself.

~Julianna

Take a step-it doesn't matter how big or how small, a step is a step. No journey can ever begin without taking a step.

~Eric

Quiet your mind and listen. If you are awakened at all hours in the night and early mornings, take time to write down the thoughts going through your head. Some of my best poetry and ideas presented themselves at those golden hours before sunrise. Make time for yourself to do what you love. Create a place you can call your own and designate a specific time to visit that place. Announce it to everyone that needs to know so they can come to expect that to be your time. Know your importance, know you are worthy, what you do does matter.

~Kim B.

Read...read anything you can get your hands on and you have an interest in. Knowledge is power on all levels. Practice these things you read and learn. Get involved with a conscious group of people. Conscious goes beyond psychic. Being conscious is a great way to live your life...awakened and aware. Be yourself no matter what in all situations. Be true to you! Explore...play...the Universe does have a sense of humor.

~Christy

Start within and work your way. Be aware. If something attracts you, investigate. Read, ask questions, talk to knowledgeable people.
Observe...experiment...experience. Most of all, take what you need and throw the rest out. Remember, we all learn at our own pace and the best lessons learned are through experience. My journey is mine, yours is yours. They may or may not be similar.

~Toria

Read, read, read anything that truly interests you. There's many interviews on the internet of spiritual teachers--listen to them. Expose yourself to as many experiences as you can--workshops, classes, etc. You don't need to know what your path is. You only need to live and trust that you are always on your path. One day you will discover that you are doing what you love--

that is your path, and it may change over the years as you grow. One step leads to another. It is a great adventure, if you just trust that you are being led. Each morning I play, 'use me as you will'. It is a sense of freedom that occurs to know that you will be where you need to be and will meet those you need to meet. We just need to open and allow the Universe (God) to work through us.

~Jeanne

Hook up with Hay House Radio and listen to a few shows. Tune in to what is going on with Sounds True. There are two resources where you will get yourself on some fantastic email lists, which will move you into learning about many more modalities in the spiritual arena.

Or, dive right in and ask the Universe to bring you the resource about spirituality which would be best as an introduction for you. Once it arrives, digest the information and ask for more!

Or, realize you have all of the information you need inside of you and take up a meditation practice or live aware of everything going on around you and peel it apart to see the core truth within each situation. Do it your way, that is the only right way.

~Amy

Try to find other people like you. I really felt like I was understood for the first time when I went to a psychic workshop. Not only do you get to meet other people with gifts, you are also able to work on and improve the abilities you have, as well as other abilities you may not have thought to tap into.

~Kim S.

If you have a weird urge to do something out of the blue, DO IT! There is a reason for that feeling or urge. I believe that everyone has a gift. Half the fun of having a gift is exploring and finding that gift. How boring would it be if everyone just KNEW what their gift was? It's like when people ask me during a reading who their 'soul mate' is. How boring would it be if we were just all matched right away with our soul mates? Most of the fun is in the adventure of finding your soul mate and making mistakes along the way on your journey. It just makes you appreciate something so much more if you have to work for it to achieve it.

Be open, learn, explore, and embrace it!

~Breanna

Ask expansive questions. Ask your angels, spirit guides, passed loved ones, God, whomever you choose.

Here's how I explain it to help you in asking for help.

Angels, for example, can't intercede unless you ask for help. I suggest that you ask questions by using the question, 'What?'

> *What's my next step?*

> *What will bring me more clarity?*

> *What can be better than this?*

> *What's right about this?*

When we ask questions with 'What', we go into the right brain. The right brain is connected to the creative, imaginative, infinite brain and is also the easiest for the spiritual information to filter through.

When we ask questions with 'How'...How is this going to work? How am I going to do this? We go into the left brain. We can only get answers/solutions/information from whatever we have heard, seen, done or learned in this lifetime. It is very limited so our answer/solution/information is going to be very limited.

So, when you ask using the question, 'What', and we do not look to answer it, our mind, our spiritual beings are here to help us with solutions we may not have even thought possible. It is incredible!

~Kathy

Alright! We're charged up! Ready to go!

CHAPTER 8

WHAT IS MY NEXT STEP?

The first step is the one you believe in and the second one might be profound...

~Shinedown, 'I'll Follow You'

By doing what you've always done, you'll get what you've always gotten. Do something new to get something new-you don't know where you will find your 'a-ha!' moments!

You are where you are, and that is the perfect place to start from. The choices you have made and the beliefs you have are what have gotten you to where you are now, in this moment.

One choice you made was to read this book. I hope you've gathered new insights and much useful information. I am very grateful to have been a source for your expansion.

Here's a few suggestions to get you started-

-**Read:** Go to the library, download a Kindle book (some are free), find articles online that interest you, download free ebooks.

-**Take Classes:** There are many classes online you can take. Depending on where you live, there may be some New Age shops that offer classes/workshops on various topics. Some holistic healers and wellness practitioners in your area may conduct classes, too.

-**Find Groups:** This will help immeasurably to have others to discuss things with, learn from, and share. Facebook and Meetup are a couple of places to find groups, and there are many, many privately organized groups.

-**Meditate:** If you are new to it, it may take practice for you to quiet your mind. The more you do it, the easier it gets. Personally, I like guided meditations since my mind tends to wander when it starts getting quiet. There are many guided meditations online. YouTube is a great source.

-**Ask:** Ask questions that are expansive. For example, 'What am I truly capable of?'. Don't try and answer it, just send out the great vibe that comes with it, feeling so capable. Ask others about their experiences, ask the Universe, ask God. Be sure to listen for the answers, and be grateful for getting them.

-**Listen:** Listen for words that grab your attention-in a conversation, on television, in a song. There is a reason they get your attention. Listen to telesummits, podcasts, interviews. There's many knowledgeable people out there speaking on topics you are curious to know more about.

-**Research:** Search on the internet to find out more about some keywords or phrases that interest you, and see where that leads you. Explore the websites mentioned earlier.

A surprise BONUS for you! Join the secret group My Spirit, My Journey on Facebook! Another place to meet folks who are like-minded. Connect with others, share your 'a-ha' moments, ask questions, find resources. facebook.com/groups/MySpirit.MyJourney.

(Please note the 'dot' between MySpirit and MyJourney.)

You will never 'get it done'. Each thing you learn and each new experience you have will bring a thirst for more. It's not about getting to a certain place, it's about all the things you learn and experience along the way that bring the changes, the 'a-ha' moments, the joy you didn't think was possible. It's all about the journey! What's your next step?

ACKNOWLEDGEMENTS

Thank you so much to these beautiful souls who shared their experiences and advice. Some of these fine folks can be found online! Please visit their websites and learn more about them.

Eric Earll 2guysintheknow.com

Christy Steinbach fullmoonproductions.biz

Erin DeWitt ConsciousLivingNow.org

Bert Allen 2guysintheknow.com

Jeanne Marie Troge, MA mistsofthecelticheart.com

Kathy Bennett kathybennett.net

Julianna Muthu JuliannaMuthu.com

Keely Gelineau KeelyGelineau.com

Amy Cerny Vasterling, The Intuitive Pathfinder

intuitivepathfinder.com

Tammy Campy

bit.ly/YouAre-BigAffirmationsForLittleOnes

Nicole Wenner

sites.google.com/a/naturesowndesign.com/2013

Kim Buskala

Kim Spoor

Nicole Smith

Dr. Lori Cypher

Rachel Morin

Sara Bryki

Ashley Sullivan

Dakota Lasher

Angel Woodhall

Breanna

Jessica

Toria

ABOUT THE AUTHOR

Theresa Williams is a speaker, best-selling author, and new beginnings expert. She holds space for others to learn about themselves and open their mind to new ways of thinking, allowing and assisting them to be, do, and have the things in life they desire. She loves singing, playing guitar, road trips, good times with great friends and being in nature. Theresa lives in Minnesota with her husband and two dogs. Learn more at theverbalvisionary.com.

Theresa has co-authored 2 best-selling Kindle books, *Wisdom of Midlife Women 2,* and *Unleash Your Inner Magnificence,* both through Inspired Living Publishing.

Connect with Theresa through myspiritmyjourney.com.

If you'd like to receive updates, feel-good tools, and special invitations, get on the VIP list for all the latest!

Sign up at bit.ly/EmpowerVIP & get a special bonus gift.